Called by the King

Walking in the Way of Christ & the Apostles
Study Guide Series
Part 2, Book 8
A 7-Session Study

Peter Briggs

ISBN 9781947642119

Daystar

Published by:
Daystar Institute / NM, Inc.
P.O. Box 50567
Albuquerque, NM 87181
www.DaystarInstituteNM.us

Distributed in Africa by:
Daystar Institute / Africa
Kampala, Uganda
www.DaystarInstituteAfrica.org

Table of Contents

WitW
Walking in the Way of
Christ & the Apostles

Introduction

Jesus Christ, in His three-year ministry with His twelve disciples, modeled the method for teaching disciples to walk in His way.

The WitW Study Guide Series is not your usual book-by-book or topical Bible study. Rather, it uses a holistic approach to challenge students to apply biblical principles to their lives and ministries.

This study guide series is designed to equip disciples of Jesus Christ to become thoroughly established in the way of Christ and the apostles according to the Apostle Paul's mandate in Colossians 2:6-7. Our materials emphasize discipleship without compromise, practical Christian theology, and building a biblical worldview.

Bible study teachers and leaders are encouraged to read the WitW Theological Readers, Parts 1-4 (TR1-4) in order to gain a better understanding of the material presented in the WitW Study Guide Series, Parts 1-4, Books 1-17. All of the books that make up the entire WitW study are listed at the back of this study guide. These materials are available through our website or at Amazon.com

Leaders may use their discretion as to how much material to cover in any given discussion session.

Introduction to Book 8

Since the need for Christian discipleship is so great within the church today, I have prepared the Part 2, Books 8, 9, and 10 as a trilogy on the biblical representation of Christian discipleship.

Book 8 answers the question: "What does Christ's call into discipleship and the expected response to that call look like?"

Book 9 answers the question: "What is the expected fruit in a disciple's life?" Our focus is in two areas: a life thrust toward Christlikeness, and ministry identity.

Book 10 answers the question: "What developed and sustained disciplines should characterize the disciple's life from the instant of his responding to Christ's call until the end of his life?"

Join us now in this pilgrimage in uncompromising discipleship.

Book 8 Goals

1. To understand the reality and nature of Jesus' call to follow Him as disciples in our culture.

2. To respond to the call of Christ in the following ways:

   Immediate and unequivocal obedience to the call.

   Recognition of the supreme value of relationship with God through Jesus Christ.

   Attunement to the voice of Jesus Christ as Shepherd and King.

   Life thrust toward Christlikeness.

Our desire is that every disciple of Jesus Christ be firmly rooted, built up, and established in his faith in accordance with Colossians 2:6-7. We have prayerfully designed the WitW study materials to equip you with the tools and concepts needed to achieve this goal. May the word of God dwell in our hearts richly through faith by studying it, reflecting upon it, and allowing it to penetrate into the deepest recesses of our souls. By this means, we bring our hearts and minds into alignment with God's heart and mind.

As you begin each lesson, pray that God would open your heart to the study of His word, that He would speak to you through His word, and that He would cause His Holy Spirit to use the word of God to break up the fallow ground of your heart. This study is not about learning a lot of facts. It is about living out the truth of the Scripture in order to glorify God and impact others for the advancement of Christ's kingdom.

Notes & Reflections

Formulate a statement of your personal goals and objectives for this study of The Authority of the King. Also, make note of any additional insights or comments as begin this study.

Session 1. The Call of God – Part One

Called to a New Life, a New Identity, and a New Vocation

Can you imagine receiving a phone call from a king? For most people in our day and time, being contacted by a king would be an extremely improbable event. How would we respond? Most likely we would be in total disbelief, and so shocked as to be speechless.

Yet we, as believers in Jesus, have been called into a relationship with the very King of the universe in the same way that Jesus' 1st century disciples were called.

Even as was the case with His 1st century disciples, Jesus calls us to a new life, a new identity, and a new vocation.

Every disciple of Jesus Christ should consider himself to have been specifically and individually called by the King to become His follower. Christ's call is more than just a call to salvation, however. It is a call to a specific ministry identity.

God imparts to each of his children a unique set of gifts and talents that enable him to serve in specific ministry roles with great power and fruitfulness.

What does the call of God look like? To answer that question, we will examine a number of calling episodes in Scripture to note commonalities and differences among them. In particular, we will pay careful attention to the response of the individual being called.

Calling Episodes in Matthew's Gospel

Our first calling episode is recorded in the 4th chapter of Matthew's Gospel as follows:

Matthew 4:18-22. As He was walking along the Sea of Galilee, He saw two brothers, Simon, who was called Peter, and his brother

Andrew. They were casting a net into the sea, since they were fishermen. "Follow Me," He told them, "and I will make you fish for people!" Immediately they left their nets and followed Him. Going on from there, He saw two other brothers, James the son of Zebedee, and his brother John. They were in a boat with Zebedee their father, mending their nets, and He called them. Immediately they left the boat and their father and followed Him.

Q1. From this Scripture passage, what observations can we make regarding the following:

The nature of Jesus call.

The response of the four men.

The cost to themselves and their families.

The change to their self-identity and vocation.

Jesus called these fishermen as He was going about His work of ministry, seeking and saving the lost. God interrupted their world when Jesus uttered His great invitation into a relationship that completely changed their identity and their vocation. They immediately and without hesitation left their vocations and the source of their livelihoods to become those who would fish for people

Matthew 9:9-13. As Jesus went on from there, He saw a man named Matthew sitting at the tax office, and He said to him, "Follow Me!" So he got up and followed Him. While He was reclining at the table in the house, many tax collectors and sinners came as guests to eat with Jesus and His disciples. When the

Pharisees saw this, they asked His disciples, "Why does your Teacher eat with tax collectors and sinners?" But when He heard this, He said, "Those who are well don't need a doctor, but the sick do. Go and learn what this means: I desire mercy and not sacrifice. For I didn't come to call the righteous, but sinners."

Q2. From this Scripture passage, what observations can we make regarding the following:

Matthew's chosen profession.

Christ's attitude toward Matthew.

Matthew's response to Christ's call.

Evidently, Matthew hosted a banquet at his home in Jesus' honor, and his invited guests included fellow tax collectors.

Q3. How did the Pharisees respond to Matthew's gracious hospitality?

Q4. What can we observe from Jesus' response to the Pharisees' criticism?

From this Scripture passage, what observations can we make regarding the following:

Matthew's chosen profession.

Christ's attitude toward Matthew.

Matthew's response to Christ's call.

Evidently, Matthew hosted a banquet at his home in Jesus' honor, and his invited guests included fellow tax collectors.

Q5. How did the Pharisees respond to Matthew's gracious hospitality?

Q6. What can we observe from Jesus' response to the Pharisees' criticism?

Calling Episode in John's Gospel

The record of Jesus' interaction with some of His disciples recorded in the 1st chapter of John's Gospel seems to have taken place near the time when Jesus was baptized, although John doesn't mention the baptism. Therefore, this calling episode probably took place prior to the calling episodes recorded in the 4th chapter of Matthew's Gospel.

Read John 1:29-51.

Q7. Analyze the calling episode recorded in the above passage with respect to the following:

Who were the men being called by Christ?

Describe the process whereby each of these men was introduced to Christ.

How did each man respond to Jesus' call?

Calling of Zacchaeus

Jesus' interaction with Zacchaeus is recorded in the 18th chapter of Luke's Gospel. The story of Zacchaeus is a favorite of small children.

Read Luke 19:1-10.

Q8. Analyze Jesus call to Zacchaeus in regard to the following:

Zacchaeus' occupation and his position in society.

The timing and location of Jesus' call to Zacchaeus.

The manner in which Zacchaeus responded to Christ's call.

The manner in which Jesus represented His purpose in calling people to Himself.

Q9. In the calling of Zacchaeus, who was looking for whom? What do we learn from this fact?

In Jesus' encounter with Zacchaeus, we observe this noteworthy principle at work: although, from our perspective, we may feel that we are seeking God, in reality He is the One seeking us.

Calling of Paul

The calling of Paul is recorded in the 9th chapter of Acts; it is a pivotal event in the early history of the church.

Read Acts 9:1-19.

Here Luke records the conversion of Saul, who would become Paul, the great apostle to the Gentiles.

Q10. Describe the unique characteristics of Paul's call in regard to the following parameters:

Paul's spiritual condition.

It's timing relative to Christ's life and ministry.

The impact of Christ's call on the direction of Paul's life.

Read 1 Timothy 1:12-17.

Q11. How does this passage expand our understanding of Paul's conversion and his attitude toward Christ?

Where the previous calls were made during Jesus' lifetime, Christ's call to Paul occurred after His resurrection. And, praise God, He is still calling people to follow Him today.

Calling of Abraham

Read Genesis 12:1-9.

Here Moses records Yahweh's calling of Abraham, which is one of the most important and pivotal events in all of history.

Q12. Analyze the significance of Yahweh's calling of Abraham in regard to the following parameters:

Its time in history.

Its demands upon Abraham.

The nation of Israel.

Yahweh's promised blessings and curse.

We can learn at least two things from this narrative:

God has always been calling out a people to be His very own and to walk in His way.

Although the call of God demands obedience, it also promises blessing in return for obedience.

This is the essence of the Apostle Peter's assertion in the following passage from the 1st chapter of his 2nd epistle:

2 Peter 1:4. By these He has given us very great and precious promises, so that through them you may share in the divine nature, escaping the corruption that is in the world because of evil desires.

The Apostle Peter states that God has given to us, who have responded positively to His call, His very great and precious promises.

Q13. What is the result of our laying hold upon, appropriating, and practicing the very great and precious promises of God?

Q14. List some of the blessings that we receive when we heed Christ's call and become His fully devoted followers? *Hint*: Refer to the 1st chapter of Ephesians for some ideas.

Notes & Reflections

Session 2. The Call of God – Part Two

Review and Analysis

Briefly review Session 1 in which we considered several calling episodes.

Q1. Summarize the governing principles of discipleship that seem to be at work in each of the persons being called.

The fishermen, Peter, Andrew, James, and John – Matthew 4:18-22.

The tax collector, Matthew (or Levi) – Matthew 9:9-13.

Disciples of John the Baptist – John 1:29-51.

The tax collector, Zacchaeus – Luke 19:1-10.

The Pharisee, Paul – Acts 9:1-19.

Abraham, idol worshiper from Ur – Genesis 12:1-4.

Q2. List, analyze, and discuss the similarities and differences among the calling episodes we have examined thus far.

Similarities.

Differences.

Q3. Based upon your foregoing analysis, formulate a short list (no more than six items) of the key parameters displayed in all of the responses to the call of God in the examples studied thus far.

Following are some of my observations from the calling episodes we have examined:

All the persons being called seemed to recognize that they were receiving a call from God Himself, and they were immediately and wholeheartedly obedient to His call.

All experienced a total life transformation as a result of their obedience.

All experienced a radical change in identity.

All experienced a radical change of vocation.

All were called to discipleship, not merely belief.

All were sinful people prior to the call of God.

The response of some was facilitated by another person.

The call of God stretches across time, beginning with Abraham (ca. 18th century BC) and continuing to our day and time in the 21st century AD.

God is the initiator and prime mover in the calling experience; our seeking God is the result of His first seeking us.

Associated with the call of God are very great and precious promises, by which our lives increasingly radiate the glory of God.

Negative Example: The Rich Young Ruler

Briefly review Session 1 in which we considered several calling episodes.

Q4. Summarize the governing principles of discipleship that seem to be at work in each of the persons being called.

The fishermen, Peter, Andrew, James, and John – Matthew 4:18-22.

The tax collector, Matthew (or Levi) – Matthew 9:9-13.

Disciples of John the Baptist – John 1:29-51.

The tax collector, Zacchaeus – Luke 19:1-10.

The Pharisee, Paul – Acts 9:1-19.

Abraham, idol worshiper from Ur – Genesis 12:1-4.

Q5. List, analyze, and discuss the similarities and differences among the calling episodes we have examined thus far.

Similarities.

Differences.

Q6. Based upon your foregoing analysis, formulate a short list (no more than six items) of the key parameters displayed in all of the responses to the call of God in the examples studied thus far.

Following are some of my observations from the calling episodes we have examined:

All the persons being called seemed to recognize that they were receiving a call from God Himself, and they were immediately and wholeheartedly obedient to His call.

All experienced a total life transformation as a result of their obedience.

All experienced a radical change in identity.

All experienced a radical change of vocation.

All were called to discipleship, not merely belief.

All were sinful people prior to the call of God.

The response of some was facilitated by another person.

The call of God stretches across time, beginning with Abraham (ca. 18th century BC) and continuing to our day and time in the 21st century AD.

God is the initiator and prime mover in the calling experience; our seeking God is the result of His first seeking us.

Associated with the call of God are very great and precious promises, by which our lives increasingly radiate the glory of God.

Summary

Following is a summary of key observations from our study thus far:

The call of Christ brings about a radical transformation of both our identity and our vocation.

The call of God is addressed to people who recognize their sinful state before Him, not to those who are content in their self-righteousness. Living a righteous life prior to the call of God is certainly commendable, but it is not a prerequisite for receiving that call. In fact, being content in one's self-righteousness is a hindrance to responding positively to Christ's call into discipleship.

Christ's disciples introduce others to Jesus as Messiah.

There is a causative connection between God seeking us and our seeking Him, as manifested in the Zacchaeus episode.

The call of Christ into discipleship is not limited to the early 1st century AD during Jesus' life and ministry. In fact, the resurrected and ascended Christ is still calling followers to Himself in the 21st century.

Jesus Christ promises eternal blessings for those who joyfully heed His call to follow Him and submit to His authority as their King.

The risen and ascended Christ is always active, pursuing the expansion of His kingdom through the agency of the Holy Spirit. This brings Him into life-altering contact with us. When we recognize and respond to His invitation to "follow Me," we are called to self-sacrifice, discipleship, and ministry – not merely belief. We immediately experience a radical change in our identity as we become children of God. We also experience a radical change in our vocation as we become servants of God. In this connection, reflect on your personal experience of Jesus' call.

Q7. Describe how you experienced His call? What difference has it made in your lifestyle and vocation?

Q8. What external or internal influences in your life made responding to Christ's call challenging?

Q9. Which of the calling episodes we have examined in Scripture most closely represents the call of God in your own life? Discuss the rationale for your answer.

Notes & Reflections

Session 3. Responding to the Call of God – Part One

Factors which Characterize a Proper Response to the Call of God

There are four normative factors that are observed in all of the biblical examples of those who heeded the call of God and who decisively turned from their prideful rebellion to walk in His way. These factors are normative because they apply to all people, periods and places. If these four factors are not evident in a person's life, there is a strong likelihood that he has not yet responded positively to the call of God.

Immediate and unequivocal obedience to the call.

Recognition of the supreme value of relationship with God through Jesus Christ.

Attunement to the voice of Jesus Christ as Shepherd and King.

Life thrust toward Christlikeness.

Q1. List examples of each of the four factors in the calling episodes which we examined in the last session.

Would you agree that only the first two factors listed above were immediately evident in the examples we studied? But as we consider the trajectory, or thrust, of the disciple's lives after their initial call, we can clearly observe the third and fourth factors as well.

In the discussion that follows, each of the four governing principles is examined in greater detail.

Immediate and Unequivocal Obedience to the Call

This is the first normative factor that characterizes a proper response to the call of God. In thinking about immediate and unequivocal obedience, we can learn much by comparing and contrasting the directions of Peter and Paul's lives after they received the call to follow Jesus Christ as His disciple. We have already examined the calling and conversion of Paul as recorded in Acts 9.

Read Matthew 4:18-22, 14:28-32, 16:16, & 26:33-35; John 21:1-25; Acts 1:15-16, 2:14-40, 3:1-7 & 4:7-12; and Galatians 2:11-14.

Q2. Trace Peter's development after he received the call of Jesus Christ as recorded in the 4th chapter of Matthew's Gospel.

If you have a Bible concordance or a Bible database on a computer, you can search for other passages that mention Peter (***Hint***: Cephas is Peter's other name).

Q3. Compare and contrast Peter's trajectory with that of Paul.

Similarities.

Differences.

While Peter did, in fact, immediately leave all and follow Christ, he experienced episodes of doubt and wavering, even to the point of outright denial that he was one of Jesus' followers, until after Christ's resurrection. From that point onward, Peter seems to have unreservedly grasped the essence of the gospel. Except for the episode mentioned by Paul in Galatians 2:11-14, we do not observe the kind of fluctuations in Peter's commitment to the gospel that occurred prior to Christ's resurrection.

Peter, like most of us, struggled with obedience to the call of Christ on his life, whereas Paul seemingly did not. The call of God is to a life characterized by truth, righteousness, holiness, and humility. This call demands perseverance and total reliance on God's transforming power operating in our lives.

We might even say that Peter's conversion was more of a **process** whereas Paul's radical conversion was an **event**. My purpose in bringing this up is to state the following: whether or not you can point to a specific date, time, and place of your conversion, if the trajectory of your life is consistent with the four governing principles listed above, then you can be confident that you are in Christ and are destined for His eternal kingdom.

The validity of our response to the call of God is not determined by a prayer expressed or an action taken at some time in the past, but rather a life characterized by trust, obedience, and patient endurance in the present.

2 Peter 1:3-11. By these He has given us very great and precious promises, so that through them you may share in the divine nature, escaping the corruption that is in the world because of evil desires. For this very reason, make every effort to supplement your faith with **moral excellence**, moral excellence with **experiential knowledge**, experiential knowledge with **self-control**, self-control with **patient endurance**, patient endurance with **godliness**, godliness with **brotherly kindness**, and brotherly kindness with **self-sacrificing love**. For if these qualities are yours and are increasing, they will keep you from being useless or unfruitful in the knowledge of our Lord Jesus Christ. The person who lacks these things is blind and shortsighted and has forgotten the cleansing from his past sins. Therefore, brothers, make every effort to confirm your calling and election, because if you do these things you will never stumble. For in this way, entry into the eternal kingdom of our Lord and Savior Jesus Christ will be richly supplied to you. [Adapted from the HCSB]

The point of this discussion is that neither Peter's conversion experience nor that of Paul can be considered normative. While both men responded to Christ's call with immediate and unequivocal obedience, it seems to have taken Peter some time to become established in his commitment to the gospel. On the other hand, Paul seems to have become established in his commitment within days of his Damascus road experience.

Q4. Reflect on your own response to the call of Christ, and your becoming established in your commitment to the gospel. Was your experience more like that of Peter or more like that of Paul?

Notes & Reflections

Session 4. Responding to the Call of God – Part Two

Recognition of the Supreme Value of Relationship with God through Jesus Christ

This is the second normative factor that characterizes a proper response to the call of God.

To what degree do we really value our relationships, especially with those closest to us? Do you agree that we have a tendency to take others for granted, especially those whom we love the most? Often it is not until the death of a loved one that we truly appreciate all that person meant to us in life.

Our obedience to a command issued by a person in authority is largely a function of our respect for and the degree to which we value our relationship with that person.

Each of the Scripture passages either cited or quoted below reflect in some way upon the supreme value of our being citizens of Christ's kingdom, following Him as disciples, and having the position of being in Christ.

Matthew 13:44-46. The kingdom of heaven is like treasure, buried in a field, that a man found and reburied. Then in his joy he goes and sells everything that he has and buys that field. Again, the kingdom of heaven is like a merchant in search of fine pearls. When he found one priceless pearl, he went and sold everything that he had and bought it.

Q1. How does a person treat something that he regards as supremely valuable?

Read Luke 14:25-33. This passage is one of the most pointed and emphatic teachings from the lips of Jesus concerning the cost of discipleship. Later in this session, I will be quoting a portion of the passage; read the entire passage to grasp the context.

Q2. Reflect again on our discussion of the call which Christ issued to Andrew, Peter, James, John, and Matthew, as recorded in the 4th and 9th chapters of Matthew. What do their responses to Christ's call manifest in regard to their evaluation of Jesus Christ as a person and the status of being His disciple?

Philippians 3:7-11. But everything that was gain to me, I have considered to be a loss because of Christ. More than that, I consider everything to be a loss in view of the surpassing value of knowing Christ Jesus my Lord. Because of Him I have suffered the loss of all things and consider them filth, so that I may gain Christ and be found in Him, not having a righteousness of my own from the law, but one that is through the faith of Christ – the righteousness from God based on faith. My goal is to know Him and the power of His resurrection and the fellowship of His sufferings, becoming conformed to His death, assuming that I will somehow reach the resurrection from the dead. [Adapted from the HCSB]

Q3. Based upon this testimony from the pen of the Apostle Paul, how much did he value being in Christ?

Luke 14:26-27 & 33. If anyone comes to Me and does not hate his own father and mother, wife and children, brothers and sisters

– yes, and even his own life – he cannot be My disciple. Whoever does not bear his own cross and come after Me cannot be My disciple... In the same way, therefore, every one of you who does not say goodbye to all his possessions cannot be My disciple.

Q4. What poignant comparisons does Jesus make in this passage?

Our relationship with Jesus Christ must take precedence over all other relationships.

A Counter-Example: The Rich Young Ruler

In the 19th chapter of Matthew we observe a counter-example when the rich young ruler came to Jesus.

Matthew 19:20-22. "I have kept all these," the young man told him. "What do I still lack?" "If you want to be perfect," Jesus said to him, "go, sell your belongings and give to the poor, and you will have treasure in heaven. Then come, follow Me." When the young man heard that command, he went away grieving, because he had many possessions.

Q5. What do these verses communicate regarding the rich young ruler's evaluation of Jesus Christ as a person and the status of being His disciple?

It is the recognition of the supreme value of Jesus Christ as a person and the status of being His disciple that is manifested in the responses of Peter, Andrew, James, John, and Matthew. In contrast, the rich young ruler valued his possessions more than the status of being Christ's disciple.

In fact, he valued the transient things of this present life more than being a citizen of Christ's eternal kingdom. In fact, anything that stands between our hearts and Christ, upon which we have fastened our affections in preference to Christ, is an idol.

Psalm 42:1-4. As a deer longs for streams of water, so I long for You, O Yahweh. I thirst for Yahweh, the living Elohim. When can I come and appear before Yahweh? My tears have been my food day and night, while all day long people say to me, "Where is your Elohim?" I remember this as I pour out my heart: how I walked with many, leading the festive procession to the house of Yahweh, with joyful and thankful shouts. [Adapted from the HCSB]

Revelation 21:6-7. And He said to me, "It is done! I am the Alpha and the Omega, the Beginning and the End. I will give water as a gift to the thirsty from the spring of life. The one who overcomes will inherit these things, and I will be his God, and he will be My son." [Adapted from the HCSB]

Q6. The qualification for inheriting a place in Christ's eternal kingdom is to **overcome**. What is the significance of this qualification? What are we to overcome, and who or what is our example of overcoming?

Q7. What is the significance of the water metaphor in these verses in regard to our relationship to Christ?

Thirst is a powerful motivator, and failure to quench it is a life and death issue. Our thirst for water affords a picture of how passionately – even with a sense of desperation – we are to seek after and follow Christ.

Something that is missing from the lives of many professing Christians is a real passion for Christ. In fact, I believe such people are Christians in name only – people of the flesh according to Paul's terminology in the 3rd chapter of 1 Corinthians. The value we place upon our relationship with Christ is seen in the amount of time we spend actively seeking and serving Him.

Notes & Reflections

Session 5. Responding to the Call of God – Part Three

Attunement to the Voice of Jesus Christ as Shepherd and King

This is the third normative factor that characterizes a proper response to the call of God. In a society where we are bombarded by a multitude of voices, all seeking to get our attention, how can we attune ourselves to hear the voice of our Lord?

This beautiful metaphor of the sheep and the shepherd contains helpful principles for us. Following are excerpts:

John 10:4-15. ₄ When he has brought all his own outside, he goes ahead of them. The sheep follow him because they recognize his voice. ₅ They will never follow a stranger; instead they will run away from him, because they don't recognize the voice of strangers... ₁₁ I am the good shepherd. The good shepherd lays down his life for the sheep.... ₁₄ I am the good shepherd. I know My own sheep, and they know Me, ₁₅ as the Father knows Me, and I know the Father. I lay down My life for the sheep.

Q1. How do the sheep know to follow their shepherd?

Q2. Think about the significance of the shepherd / sheep metaphor. What similarities are there between the way the shepherd leads and guides his sheep with the way Christ leads and guides His disciples?

Q3. Discuss the significance of this in relation to the manner in which Jesus' disciples receive direction and guidance only from Him.

Sheep are not known for their intelligence. Left on their own, they would probably die. They need a shepherd to watch, protect, and guide them. In antiquity, the shepherd lived with his flock, taking them to pasture during the day, and to the sheepfold at night. Sheepfolds in antiquity were often enclosures made of stone, with a single opening for the entrance. The shepherd would lie down across the entrance as a barrier for animals trying to enter the fold, or sheep leaving it. Often sheepfolds were shared by a number of shepherds with their flocks. Yet each sheep recognized his own shepherd's voice and followed only that particular shepherd and no other. Likewise the shepherd knew his own flock.

In our world, there are a multitude of voices that clamor for our attention and seek to give us guidance and direction.

Q4. What are some of these other voices that are competing with the voice of your Shepherd?

Q5. How do we become trained to respond to the voice of our Shepherd. What disciplines are involved in this training?

According to Henry Blackaby in his book, *Experiencing God*, [1] there are four ways in which God communicates with us. Recognizing these four ways helps to remove some of the complexity and mystery associated with our hearing the voice of God.

1. God's Word. Scripture is the primary means by which God speaks and gives direction to His people. Therefore, it is essential that we constantly bathe our minds in Scripture. If the other three ways seem to lead in a direction contrary to the clear teaching of Scripture, they should be rejected.

2. Listening Prayer. Prayer is a two-way conversation in which we not only present our prayers of intercession, supplication, and thanksgiving before God's throne of grace, but also the Holy Spirit can respond to our requests for wisdom by bringing Scripture passages, biblical principles, or even very specific direction to mind, thus providing profound insight and direction.

3. Circumstances. God leads or directs us through circumstances, both positive and negative.

4. Godly Counsel. God often speaks through the wisdom of His people. Seek out godly counsel from a wise saint of God. The fact that sin is, by definition, deceitful means that it is often very difficult, if not impossible, for us to see the snares that lie in wait for us. We desperately need other believers who are willing to hold us accountable and ask the hard questions to help, encourage, and exhort us to resolutely walk in the way of Christ and the apostles. However, as vitally important as godly counsel is, it is of utmost importance that we check that counsel against the clear teachings of Scripture to ensure that it is, in fact, godly.

There are two passages of Scripture that we are going to analyze with regard to the manner in which the people of God received guidance. The first is the 37th through 50th chapters of Genesis, which focus primarily upon Joseph and the complex relationship he had with his brothers. The second is the 16th chapter of Acts, which records the 2nd missionary expedition of the Apostle Paul and his team.

Q6. Embracing Henry Blackaby's four avenues of receiving divine guidance, identify which ones apply to each of the passages below.

The Joseph story, Genesis 37 – 50.

Paul's 2nd Missionary Expeditions, Acts 16.

Both of these passages illustrate the importance of circumstances in determining the will of God.

Q7. List other biblical passages that support each of the four avenues of receiving divine guidance. The passages you select can come from any literary genre; in other words, they can be teaching passages or ones that illustrate divine guidance in action.

Q8. Describe a situation in which you desired to know the will of God. By what means did you determine what His will was? To what extent did your approach to determining God's will correspond with Blackaby's model? What was the outcome?

Q9. How would you go about instructing and counseling people to practice Blackaby's model for knowing and doing the will of God?

Two things need to be kept in mind. First, the clear teaching of Scripture always take precedence over prayer, circumstances, and godly counsel. God will never contradict the words of Scripture when read and interpreted in accordance with the principles that we learned from Book 4 in Part 1 of the WitW study. There are many spirits in the world seeking to lead us astray if we are not attuned to the Spirit of truth.

Secondly, God does not speak through our emotions. Our emotions are never a reliable indicator of the will of God. That said, following God's leading often results in deep peace, a supernatural fruit of the Holy Spirit.

We can only hear from God if we are attuned to His voice and if we are committed to doing His will. His voice is not an audible one, but rather comes to us as we search the Scripture and allow God to speak to us through His word and His spirit. The more we respond to His voice, the easier it becomes for us to hear it.

Concluding Remarks with regard to Knowing and Doing the Will of God

Often our reason for wanting to hear from God is in the context of making a critical decision – in other words, a decision that will substantially affect the future trajectory of our lives. When faced with such a decision, how can we be certain that we are receiving clear direction from our Heavenly Father? I suggest the following, which reflect Henry Blackaby's model for knowing and doing the will of God:

Seek out and walk in that purpose for which God created you in accordance with Ephesians 2:8-10.

Habitually practice Proverbs 3:5-7 and James 1:5-7. Be absolutely committed to obeying and practicing the will of God once He has revealed it to you.

Habitually read and study the Bible. Maintain a discipline of reading through the entire Bible at least once every year, and practice Joshua 1:8. This includes memorizing Scripture and reciting it aloud.

Habitually practice the discipline of prayer, including intercession for the needs of others, supplication for your own needs, specific requests for wisdom, and thanksgiving for all the manifestations of God's grace toward you.

By practicing the foregoing disciplines, you will be equipped to perceive God's expression of His will through circumstances.

Seek counsel from trusted brothers and sisters in Christ to help you perceive the will of God for a critical decision.

Henry Blackaby's model for knowing and doing the will of God is balanced and effective if practiced in the context of a life that is saturated with the language of Scripture and is habitually committed to obedience.

Notes & Reflections

Session 6. Responding to the Call of God – Part Four

Life Thrust Toward Christlikeness

This is the fourth normative factor that characterizes a proper response to the call of God. In all the biblical examples of an affirmative response to God's call, we observed a definite and profound lifestyle change. Each person turned from his selfishness and pride toward submission to Christ's rule and progress toward a Christlike character. While we will never attain sinless perfection in this life, it is the goal to which we consistently aspire, and to which we constantly press forward.

Read Philippians 3:8-21. A portion of this passage is quoted below; read the entire passage to grasp the context.

Philippians 3:12-16. Not that I have already reached the goal or am already fully mature, but I make every effort to take hold of it because I also have been taken hold of by Christ Jesus. Brothers, I do not consider myself to have taken hold of it. But one thing I do: Forgetting what is behind and reaching forward to what is ahead, I pursue as my goal the prize promised by God's heavenly call in Christ Jesus. Therefore, all who are mature should think this way. And if you think differently about anything, God will reveal this also to you. In any case, we should live up to whatever truth we have attained.

Q1. What caused Paul to pursue with such zeal and tenacity God's heavenly call in Christ Jesus?

In their writings, the apostles frequently employed the metaphor of an athletic contest to portray the true character of the life of a disciple of Christ. In the passage quoted above, Paul alludes to the marathon race.

Q2. Why is the marathon race a useful representation of the Christian life?

In order to be successful in their sport, athletes must devote a tremendous amount of time and energy to training. Regrettably, many people who profess to be Christ followers take their faith for granted and do not train themselves adequately.

The following four passages exemplify the apostles' emphasis on the need for training and equipping in order to live successfully as a Christ follower:

2 Timothy 2:15. Be diligent to present yourself approved to God, a worker who doesn't need to be ashamed, correctly handling the word of truth. [Adapted from the HCSB]

2 Timothy 3:16-17. All Scripture is God-breathed, and is profitable for teaching, for rebuking, for correcting, for training in righteousness, so that the man of God may be complete, equipped for every good work. [Adapted from the HCSB]

1 Peter 3:15. ... But honor the Messiah as Lord in your hearts. Always be ready to give a defense to anyone who asks you for a reason for the hope that is in you. However, do this with gentleness and respect, keeping your conscience clear, so that when you are accused, those who denounce your Christian life will be put to shame. For it is better to suffer for doing good, if that should be God's will, than for doing evil.

2 Peter 1:3-11. His divine power has given us everything required for life and godliness through the knowledge of Him who called us by His own glory and moral excellence. By these He has given us very great and precious promises, so that through them you may share in the divine nature, escaping the corruption that is in the world because of evil desires. For this very reason, make every effort to supplement your faith with moral excellence, moral excellence with experiential knowledge, experiential knowledge with self-control, self-control with patient endurance, patient endurance with godliness, godliness with brotherly kindness, and brotherly kindness with self-sacrificing love. For if these qualities are yours and are increasing, they will keep you from being useless or unfruitful in the knowledge of our Lord Jesus Christ. The person who lacks these things is blind and shortsighted and has forgotten the cleansing from his past sins. Therefore, brothers, make every effort to confirm your calling and election, because if you do these things you will never stumble. For in this way, entry into the eternal kingdom of our Lord and Savior Jesus Christ will be richly supplied to you. [Adapted from the HCSB]

It is noteworthy that the Greek word translated "correctly handling" in 2 Timothy 2:15 is *orthotomeo*, which literally means to cut straight lines.

Q3. In accordance with the teaching of Paul and Peter, why should we diligently train ourselves in the Scriptures?

We will explore more fully the concept of a life-thrust toward Christlikeness in Book 9 in the WitW Study Guide Series.

Notes & Reflections

Session 7. Review and Discussion Questions

For many people who profess to be Christians, the experience of Christian conversion is disconnected from a call into discipleship. In fact, even as Jesus called each of His followers to enter into a specific ministry partnership with Himself, in like manner He is calling out disciples in our day and time, not simply to receive salvation from sin, but rather to enter into a specific ministry partnership with Himself.

In order to better understand the reality and nature of Jesus' call to follow Him, we looked at a number of calling episodes from the Bible, most of which resulted in positive responses. Tragically, not everyone responded favorably to God's call. Most of the positive accounts included four factors in common, which we have designated as normative principles, since they apply to all people, periods, and places; they are listed below:

Immediate and unequivocal obedience to the call.

Recognition of the supreme value of relationship with God through Jesus Christ.

Attunement to the voice of Jesus Christ as Shepherd and King.

Life thrust toward Christlikeness.

In our discussion of the third factor, we took note of Henry Blackaby's model for knowing and experiencing the will of God:

He reveals His will primarily through Scripture.

He reveals His will through listening prayer.

He reveals His will through circumstances.

He reveals His will through godly counsel.

The first avenue of knowing and experiencing the will of God through habitually reading, studying, meditating upon, and reciting Scripture in accordance with Yahweh's instruction to Joshua in Joshua 1:8 takes precedence over the other three avenues.

The call of God into a specific ministry partnership with His Son, Jesus Christ, is never simply a call to intellectually embrace the facts of the Christian gospel. Instead, it is a call to obedient and worshipful discipleship, which includes development in the seven virtues of the Christian life enumerated by the Apostle Peter in 2 Peter 1:3-11. These characteristics are imbedded in the four principles we have identified above. You may think of others.

Determining God's will for our lives requires hearing from God in the four ways outlined above, keeping in mind that emotions are not listed as a viable means of guidance or direction.

In responding to God's call:

Our identity is changed; we become children of God.

Our vocation is changed; we become servants of the living God called into a specific ministry partnership with Him.

Our motivation in life is changed; with Paul we press on to the prize of God's heavenly call in Christ Jesus.

Discussion Questions

Q1. Share your testimony of how you experienced Christ's call into discipleship. Did your call include a specific ministry partnership with Jesus Christ as Lord and King?

Q2. Describe your personal experience regarding each of the four normative principles as follows:

Immediate and unequivocal obedience to the call.

Recognition of the supreme value of relationship with God through Jesus Christ.

Attunement to the voice of Jesus Christ as Shepherd and King.

Life thrust toward Christlikeness.

Q3. In what specific areas in your life have you discarded old habits of thinking, speaking, and behaving and have replaced them with new, godly habits?

Q4. How can you use the result of our discussions in Book 8 to enhance your ministry to people to reaffirm and deepen their commitment to walking as a disciple of Christ?

Notes & Reflections

Congratulations! You are now ready to proceed to Book 9, the *Meaning of Discipleship*.

Afterword

About Us

WitW is a product of Daystar Institute of Biblical Theology and Leadership Development (DI), which is dedicated to supporting local churches in fulfillment of their mission of making disciples of all nations. We have two offices: DI / NM is based in Albuquerque, New Mexico, and DI / A is based in Kampala, Uganda. Please do not hesitate to contact us at www.DaystarInstitute/NM.us if you have any questions or comments or wish to request training in the use of our materials.

Peter Briggs is founder and president-emeritus of Daystar Institute of Biblical Theology & Leadership Development. In addition to teaching and mentoring, Dr. Briggs has authored the WitW Study Guide Series to challenge students in uncompromising discipleship, practical Christian theology, and building a biblical worldview. The WitW study has had a great impact in both East Africa and the USA and is an excellent tool for encouraging and equipping disciples of Jesus to actually live out their faith.

Dedication

The *Walking in the Way of Christ & the Apostles Study Guide Series* is dedicated to Reverend Morris Wanje, whose prayers for God to raise up a means for strengthening and equipping young pastors and church leaders in East Africa caused the Holy Spirit of God to move upon the hearts of godly men and women at Daystar Institute/NM to create this study.

Acknowledgments

I am grateful for the heroic efforts of our team of contributors, editors, board of directors, and all who have had a part in the development of the WitW study. In particular, I extend my heartfelt gratitude to my wife, Rosemarie, our daughter, Ruthanne Hamrick, and ministry associates John & Marcie Kinzer, Stephen Patterson, and Michael & Antoninah Mutinda, for their valuable input and help with the Study Guide Series; and to Darienne Dumas and Emily Fuller for proof-reading the texts.

Testimonials

"The *Walking in the Way of Christ & the Apostles* (WitW) series by Dr. Peter Briggs is a powerful tool for fulfilling Jesus' universal mandate to make disciples. WitW is theologically sound, conceptually brilliant, and life-changing for those who are trained by it. The impact of WitW is not only personal transformation into the image of Christ, but also a profound influence on families, churches, and the larger culture, whether in America or Africa or anywhere else. Peter Briggs is a theologian of substantial import, but he has not merely plied his theological craft in the halls of academia. With God's enablement, he has managed to translate biblical truth and disciple-making principles into something that actually works in the real world! Those who embrace and employ *Walking in the Way* in their own lives will find themselves part of a movement affecting generations to come."

Steven Collins, PhD,
Executive Dean, Trinity Southwest University

"*Walking in the Way of Christ & the Apostles* (WitW) is a magnificent literary work in biblical theology that offers the student an education in practical Christianity. The WitW study was first introduced in November 2011; since that time we have been using it to instruct ministry leaders and rural pastors at a low cost, and the transformation of lives is phenomenal. Learners get to understand the message of the Bible and are able to study it effectively. In my own interaction with the material since 2012, I have come to realize that Jesus Christ is using it to revive His remnant in Kenya and other parts of Africa, teaching us how to think in a biblical way and be successful in all spheres of life. I am convinced that the WitW material holds the key to Africa's revival, and, in Yahweh's hand, it is a mighty tool for returning the continent back to Him."

Michael Mutinda,
Team Leader, Daystar Institute / Africa

Walking in the Way of Christ and the Apostles
Study Guide Series (SGs)

Part 1 – Foundational Concepts. These concepts are foundational to equip the Christ-follower to have and to be governed by the mind of Christ.

1.   The Way of God
2.   The Storyline of the Bible
3.   Biblical Reality
4.   Discovering the Meaning of Scripture
5.   Torah: The Fountainhead of Wisdom
6.   The Two-Part Christian Gospel

Part 2 – The Gospel of the Kingdom of God. Here we explore the ways in which the Christian gospel confronts the prideful rebellion of the human heart and exalts Christ as King over all.

7.   Authority of the King
8.   Called by the King
9.   Meaning of Discipleship
10. Disciplines of the Kingdom
11. Household of the King
12. Second Coming of the King

Part 3 – The Gospel of God. This final set explores how the Christian gospel affords a complete solution to human depravity and the threefold problem of evil, sin, and death.

13. Introduction to the Gospel of God
14. Reason for the Gospel of God
15. Content of the Gospel of God
16. Perversions of the Gospel of God
17. Application of the Gospel of God

Theological Readers (TRs)
TR1 – Part 1: Foundational Concepts
TR2 – Part 2: The Gospel of the Kingdom of God
TR3 – Part 3: The Gospel of God
TR4 – Resources and Appendices

Theological Handbooks (THs)
TH1 – Walking in the Way
TH2 – TBD
TH3 - TBD

Connect with us at www.DaystarInstituteNM.us, or
Contact us via email at WalkingintheWayUSA@gmail.com

---

[1] Refer to Blackaby & King (2008).

www.ingramcontent.com/pod-product-compliance
Lightning Source LLC
Chambersburg PA
CBHW071935020426
42331CB00010B/2879